Decide
Your
Destination

And 42 Other Life Lessons from a Dad

By Chad Merrill

Printed in the United States of America

First Printing, 2016

ISBN: 978-1537569970

Cover and book design: Hannah Mae Miners

Author:
Chad Merrill
174 Carroll Street SE
Atlanta, GA 30312

To my sons,
Barrett and Christian.

I want you to know this:

I love you. You have unlimited potential to do anything in life. You have the permission to dream and follow your passions. I will always support you. Continue to live with intentionality and have the most fulfilling life possible. Continue to seek God's will, look to your values and make sure you are living the life you want to be living. I will always be there cheering you on.

I Love You,
Dad
Jeremiah 29:11

Table of Contents

Acknowledgements.

I am grateful to those who continue to teach and mentor me every day and to those who introduced me to all of the concepts in this book. All I have learned and all that is in this book is a result of others who shared their lives with me. I hope that I can give to others what has been given to me.

First I would like to thank my parents, Brett & Susan Merrill and my wife's parents, Pete & Jo Boatright for giving me love and support for almost 50 years. I have learned much and have been inspired by you. To Robin who has been my best friend and greatest supporter for over 30 years. We formed our values & life's mission together and she loves me both when I live them and when I stray from them. Thank you to my boys, Barrett & Christian who were the inspiration for this book; it is a privilege to be your father. Thank you to the rest of our family who has always been there for me.

Many people have played the part of mentors and encouragers along the way. Notably Jim Moye & Zoe Hicks have been central to Robin &

I along our journey. Robb Borden & my partners at Onepath made an indelible impression on how I conduct business & integrate with life. Jeremie Kubicek, Steve Cockram and the GIANT team have had a profound impact on how I use my influence for others.

In writing a book, especially a first book, there are many people who are a part of the team who make it possible. A big thank you to Joe Bunting, Kellie McGann & the Story Cartel team. Your coaching, advice, editing and help in navigating the process was invaluable. I am thankful to all who helped me to proofread, edit & critique; especially Hank & Barbara Kimmel – real writers & the best neighbors.

Introduction.

You are searching for something. You're searching for meaning, purpose, and a way to make your lives count. This hunt is reflected in the top Google searches over the last ten years. Despite living in the age of technology, some answers can't be found on the internet. The meaning and purpose you're looking for will be different from the meaning and purpose I'm looking for—we all have different callings—but the pathway to this meaning and purpose is through intentionality and journey.

You want your life to count. You want to make a difference in the world. But how? What do you do? Where do you start? The options are endless. But the road to accomplishing your dreams is paved with intentionality. Living life by accident won't get you to where you want to go.

Imagine with me that you are twenty years older. Someone asks you, "What did you want to do after you graduated?" You think back and remember the feeling. There were endless possibilities and countless dreams you wanted to accomplish. But one of two things happened. You either lived intentionally to reach those goals and create the life you wanted, or you lived life by accident, letting life happen to you as you watched your dreams fade into distant hopes.

I don't mean to be dramatic, but that really is what can happen. If you are not intentional about what direction you want to go, you'll end up somewhere you never intended.

And now the question is in the present, "What do you want to do?"

In front of you are two paths.

Accidental Living

Accidental living is easy to do. It's easier than we realize because most of us are already doing it.

This looks like letting life happen to you, rather than you controlling where you want to take your life. It's getting an easy, convenient job that pays the bills, while not taking any steps toward where you want to be in the future.

Accidental living isn't necessarily wrong; you can still accomplish a lot of great things accidentally.

But the most successful people never live their lives accidentally.

Intentional Living

The second path you can take is that of intentional living. Living intentionally is knowing where you are now and where you want to go. It's taking your long-term goal and breaking it into small steps that are really attainable.

Intentional living means action. It means taking all of your hopes and dreams and making them realities by doing them. It is the road less traveled. The journey takes courage and conviction, but the reward is a life of excitement and fulfillment.

How I Found My Mission

To live intentionally, you have to know what you want. It wasn't until I discovered what I wanted, that I could shape where I wanted to go.

When my wife, Robin, and I initially came across the concept of intentional living, we jumped at the idea. But we quickly found that in order to live intentionally, we needed to decide what we were going to live for. How would we create our plan if we lacked a destination?

So with a blank white board, Robin, our boys and I began to write a few words down that we wanted our family to be about. After a few hours of narrowing down our core ideals we came up with three phrases we believed encompassed our family's mission. As we uncovered these statements, we reminded ourselves not to just think of where we were at the time, but where we wanted to be as a family.

We re-wrote the phrases on a blank page with a black permanent marker and circled the words.

Glorify God. Love One Another. Celebrate Life's Adventures.

From that day, these three phrases shaped what we did, where we invested our time, and how we spent our money.

Glorify God.

To glorify God is our first and greatest mission. We glorify God in the way we choose to live our life. We glorify God in how we spend our time and use our resources.

There are infinite ways God is glorified in our lives. When Glorifying God is a lens through which you view your everyday life, then your thoughts, words and actions will begin to reflect this.

Every circumstance is an opportunity to glorify God. The days you get a flat tire and the days you get a promotion at work are both opportunities to glorify God. The decision to make God the center of each situation and acknowledge his presence is how we live our mission.

John Piper, a well-known pastor, tells us, "God is most glorified in us, when we are most satisfied in Him."

Love One Another.

Jesus' second and most important commandment behind his first was to love one another. A friend of mine says, "Love is to fight for the highest possible good in the life of another." Throughout my marriage I have seen that to be true. You need to see love as an intentional act and a continuous pursuit.

To love one another is to fight for one another, to persevere and never give up.

To love one another has not always come naturally to me. I've had to come to the realization that love isn't always a feeling. You'll need to discover that on your own too. Love will sometimes look more like an action than a feeling, and hopefully love will become a way of life for you.

Celebrate Life's Adventures.

You need to learn to see the circumstances in your life as an adventure. Of course overseas travel and cross-country road trips are adventures, but so is going to college, getting your first job, getting an apartment, and moving to a new city. Not only should you embrace these adventures, but I believe you need celebrate them as well.

I hope you find reason to celebrate each day, in each new and difficult situation. Celebrating life's adventures means you've been given more opportunities. Helen Keller said, "Life is either a daring adventure or nothing." I hope you long for adventure. I hope you discover new places, explore possibilities, and create incredible memories. The world is full of adventures waiting to unfold—it's up to you to pursue them.

A Note on Doing What You Want

I know it's easy for me to write, "Decide your destination. Follow your dreams. Pursue your passions." But it's a lot harder to actually live that because honestly, who knows exactly what they want to do right after they graduate? I didn't, and I still don't.

The secret is: Decide a destination now, and you'll figure out the rest along the way. It's all about the journey.

Five years into being a missionary you might realize you want to start a business. A few years after that you might find yourself dreaming of opening a coffee shop.

It's hard to know what you want to do for the rest of your life when you're in your twenties, and I'm telling you, you don't need to know exactly what you'll do.

But you should figure out what's important to you—your values—because in order to make an impact in the world, you need to know what you stand for as a person, and eventually as a family. Once you find those things, you can begin to be intentional with your choices and how you shape your life.

Discover Your Values

Making decisions is hard. As a young person, it can often feel even harder. It can feel like every decision you make as a young person will change the course of your entire life. And, actually, a lot of those decisions do. In the years ahead, you will choose a career, decide where you want to live, and maybe even find a spouse. Those are huge moments and decisions in your life.

If you're like I was, you'll want to keep as many options open as possible, terrified of making the wrong decision.

But throughout 30 years of making "life-altering" decisions, I've found that it is possible to determine which choices are best and make decisions without fear. I want to share with you the key I've relied upon for decades: my values.

A value is a principle that guides your decision-making. Values are how you judge what is important in life. Values are the guiding force in our relationships, career, spiritual lives, and how we spend our time and money. In short, our values determine how we live our lives.

Whether or not you define them, everyone has them.

The danger in not identifying your values is that you won't be aware of what's guiding your decision-making. When you don't know your values, you are more likely to make choices that you don't really want to make or even realize you're making.

I recently spent time with someone who hadn't defined her values, a woman in her 40's who had lost her direction in life. She wasn't happy with her job, so she quit. She didn't know what she wanted to do, and she spent months trying to figure it out. During that time, she grew discouraged and confused. She also began accumulating credit card debt. A few months later, this middle-aged woman had to move into her parents' house.

She was so lost because she didn't know who she was or what she wanted to do. She didn't take the time to discover her values first and it almost destroyed her life.

You see, values will define what you do, but more importantly, they will shape who you are and who you become. In time, your values will change. As you grow, move away, and start a family, you'll find you prioritize new aspects of your life.

When you're younger with less responsibility you might value travel and adventure. As you get older, your values might change to legacy and family.

When you have these values, you can do great things.

My goal as a father is to equip my sons to

accomplish their dreams while staying true to their values. So a few months ago, I decided to help my sons discover their own values.

My wife and I took our two sons to a hotel in the city. It was Christmas time and the city was covered in colorful lights and red bows, but we hadn't come to sightsee. I had an entire weekend of self-discovery planned for us.

Honestly, I wasn't sure how my sons would respond. I knew how vital it is to understand your values—but I also remembered what I was like at ages 18 and 22. At that age, I had no interest in planning my future, and I could hardly blame my sons if they felt the same way.

But time goes so fast, and this would be one of the last weekends I would get to spend with my sons before they moved away. If there was anything I wanted to help my sons discover before they left, it was a set of values to guide them.

When we got to the hotel, I found an empty conference room to set up.

My wife and sons joined me in the conference room and I gave them a few worksheets I had created earlier that week.

To my surprise, they took the exercise seriously and seemed to actually enjoy it. What we discovered that day ended up greatly impacting the vision they and our family had for the future.

I could tell they wanted to do something great

with their lives. They knew if they wanted to do great things, they needed to know what they stood for, what they valued.

Because I believe you want to do something great with your life too, I want to share with you how to identify your values.

LESSON Nᵒ. ONE:
Know Yourself.

Knowing yourself is the beginning of all wisdom.
—Aristotle

Behind every successful person is someone who knows who they are and what they want out of life. A huge part of knowing yourself is defining your values.

I've seen the impact knowing—or not knowing—one's values can have in my life and the lives of others. When you don't know what you value, it's easy to forget who you want to be and why you do what you do. Over time, you'll lose sight of your goals, getting caught up in the mundane details of daily tasks and gradually becoming discouraged. Eventually, you'll find yourself wondering how you ended up in this place and questioning whether life has purpose and meaning at all.

But when you know what you value, you have purpose. When you wake up every day knowing exactly what you stand for, you become more confident in where you're going. You're motivated to get out of bed and work toward your goals, and you are ultimately able to accomplish much more. There's an amazing difference between a person who wakes up knowing the values they live by and someone who doesn't.

Before you read any further, take some time now to identify your values. This simple exercise is the most important thing I can give you as a dad. When you base your life around the values you stand for, your potential is unlimited.

For help identifying your values head to www.decideyourdestination.com for a quiz and downloadable worksheets.

LESSON N°. TWO:
Dare to Dream.

Whatever you dream of doing, dream it bigger.
There will be skeptics who tell you to be realistic.
Ignore them.
You can do more than other people believe you can,
But you can never do more than you believe you can.

I remember the first time I dreamed big, I was in college and started a travel company out of my dorm room. My business partners and I went to a travel conference one weekend and the facilitator asked us, "What's your goal?"

I told him, "We want to do $500,000 of business every week."

The facilitator stared at me, confused. "Well, let's try and be realistic…"

He went on, but I stopped listening. I had envisioned building a company with multiple offices in multiple states and I didn't want to listen to this guy tell me it wasn't possible.

I stuck to my big dream—and a few years later, it came true.

Dream big despite what others tell you. Dream big because it's the only way you'll achieve those dreams.

What will it look like for you?

The beauty of it is that you can do anything. But whatever you dream of doing, dream it bigger. Start a company. Build a school in Costa Rica. Play college basketball. Become a social innovator. Travel to all seven continents.

You can do a lot more than your culture, or your friends, or even your teachers say you can do.

I wrote about dreaming big first because it is a vital foundation for all that you can and will do in life. When you combine your big dreams with the truth Paul writes in Philippians 4:13, "I can do all things through Christ who strengthens me," you have an unbelievably exciting future.

I want you to take a few minutes and a sheet of paper and start to dream about what you want to achieve in life for yourself, your family, God, your community, and your world. Think big.

Right now it might be to make an "A" in a class, go on a mission trip, or get a job. But always keep expanding your dreams. The "A" in math might turn out to be a Masters in Business Administration. The mission trip may turn into building a school in Costa Rica. Your innovative idea may be a billion dollar company.

Write down your dreams, read them often, and believe you can do even more.

LESSON Nº. THREE:

You Can Change a Plan, But You Need One First.

Don't let your fear of making the wrong decision stop you from making any decision.

Create a plan and you will find your destination along the way.

When I was in my early-20's I had a desk job. I remember one day sitting in my office, staring out the window, and dreaming about all the other things I wanted to do.

I thought of starting more businesses. I dreamed of incorporating my passions into something I could make money with. When I realized I spent more time staring out the window than working at the job I had, I thought, "Maybe it's time to change my plan."

Before this moment, my plan was to climb the

corporate success ladder. But what I didn't realize was just because I had this plan, it didn't mean I couldn't change it.

Figuring out life as a young adult feels terrifying. Some young people decide on a different career path every week. I've often heard people describe the process in terms like these: "I wanted to be a lawyer for a few weeks, then a writer, then a pastor, then a doctor. Then I thought I might just end up homeless."

And the thing is, not knowing is **okay.** Actually, not knowing is **normal**.

What's not okay is letting the fear of making the wrong decision stop you from moving altogether. Just because you start in one direction doesn't mean you can't change; the key is starting.

You need a plan. A ship without a rudder has no direction, and you also can't turn a ship that isn't moving.

You need a plan because that's the only way you will figure out what you actually want to do. If you don't have a plan to get somewhere, you'll end up anywhere.

Look back at your values, your passions, and the things you enjoy. Your plan should be birthed out of those things.

If you dream of being a pastor but know you need to eat, take a small step toward your dream. Get a job at Starbucks while you volunteer at a local church. Work toward your plan.

I would never have started and acquired 40 different business if I didn't have the job where I stared out the window. Taking steps in life is the only way to figure out where you want to go.

And don't limit your plans to your professional life: planning for your personal goals is important, too. If you're not intentional about going to college, saving money, or creating good friendships, these things won't happen.

So take a risk and create a plan to follow your passion. True life is found in the transitions and course corrections. Through these experiences you will discover what you *really* want to do, but more importantly, you will discover **who you are**.

LESSON N°. FOUR:
Don't Procrastinate.

You may delay, but time will not. —Ben Franklin

I had three weeks to work on a project for my International Business class. Somehow, the night before it was due, I found myself staring at a blank page. I shook my head, sighed deeply, and wished I hadn't waited until the last minute.

We've all been there.

If you're like me, sometimes it feels like the weeks or days you have to work on your projects fly by before you realize how little time you have. Other times you're fully aware of the time passing by as you deliberately avoid the projects.

I've struggled with procrastination for years. I've experienced not only the stress it causes, but something worse: by procrastinating, I've let down the people I really cared about.

A few years ago, my wife, Robin, asked me to change the tires on her car before a trip she was going to take. She asked me weeks before her trip. Every time I planned to change the tires, something came up and ultimately, I got busy and forgot. I continued to procrastinate, thinking I would get it done tomorrow. The day before the trip the tires were still not changed and Robin was very upset.

Her words still sting in my memory: "Your lack of follow through tells me you do not value the safety of me or our kids. It also shows me you don't appreciate or value my time."

While changing the tires was a seemingly small task, my procrastination left me with unintended, yet harsh consequences. She was hurt, and I felt awful. The time I spent doing other things was not at all worth the hurt it caused.

I know learning not to procrastinate might be hard for you. I used to think procrastination was just the way I worked. If you're like me, you'll even say you work better under pressure. But more often than not, procrastination leads to a lot of unnecessary stress and a lower quality product in the end. For the sake of others and yourself, learn to complete your tasks without procrastinating.

When you let down the people you care about because you procrastinated, it is one of the worst feelings. Don't let your temporary comfort of putting off your responsibilities hurt those around you.

You really can get better at planning in

advance and not procrastinating. There are hundreds of different ways to give yourself more accountability and the tools needed to schedule your time better.

Planning in advance will help you create a better product and will leave a margin in case things go wrong close to your deadline. We will talk about being a leader in other chapters, and in order to lead well, you also need to overcome procrastination.

Overcoming procrastination is a journey. It's more about learning how you work best and the importance of following through. Figuring these things out will take time.

Take the time to get to know yourself so you can discover how to make the most of your time.

LESSON N°. FIVE:
Step Back.

> *Take a step back, evaluate what is important, and enjoy life.* —*Teri Garr*

Life is busy. The years slip by while we're hardly paying attention, caught up with meetings, dinner plans, and weekend trips.

You'll start off pursuing your dreams, but as time goes by, sometimes your interests and life situation will change. People change. You will change and that's okay.

As I pursued some dreams of mine, I started a new division of Onepath, a company that helps businesses lead and operate more efficiently through the use of technology. When I first started, I loved it. But one day, I looked around at what I was doing and realized eight years had gone by. I found myself going through the motions of work and losing passion with each passing day.

I knew I needed to do something, so I took a

step back. I took some time off and re-evaluated what I was doing. As I looked at my values and goals for the next phase of my life, it became clear what I was doing then wasn't where I wanted to be.

Making a change is okay and even normal. And more important, it's the only way you can ensure you get where you want to go.

Making that change in my life allowed me to focus on what was important to me and gave me the freedom to proactively and intentionally shape the next phase of my life. The change was essential to unlocking passion and potential in my life again. It even led me to write a book.

I would never have made this change if I hadn't taken the time to step back and re-evaluate what I wanted in life.

As a pilot, I learned valuable lessons in navigation. For every one degree off you are in your navigation, you will miss your target by 92 feet for every mile you travel. It might not sound like a lot, but if you leave Atlanta going to Los Angeles, you would end up 35 miles into the Pacific Ocean rather than LAX. If you are 2 or 3 or 4 degrees off, you end up in Mexico. This is what it looks like when you don't take the time to step back.

I wrote earlier about boldly making decisions and following your dreams. You can't do those things successfully unless you are doing this as well. This is how you can correct your course and make adjustments to where you're headed. Taking time and stepping back from your everyday life to evaluate is the only way to ensure you don't end up somewhere you don't want to be.

No matter whether you run a business or serve in a ministry in Uganda, at some point you'll find your life has become busy and mundane. You have to remember to step back to remember why you're doing these things and dream of even greater possibilities.

As you pursue your dreams, remember change is healthy and natural, and every now and then, **take a step back to re-evaluate your life.**

LESSON Nº. SIX:
Start Investing Early.

Finances are more than dollar signs and percentages.

Your finances are an opportunity to either destroy or propel your future.

To be faithful with what you have now will give you more control later.

Here's some practical advice, a little Finance 101.

If you start investing $300 a month when you are 22 years old, after forty years, at eight percent interest, you will have over a million dollars. That is the power of compound interest.

But start just 10 years later and you will gain just $450,000, less than half that amount. Then, you'll have to invest $700 just to reach the same result.

The more you invest and the earlier you invest it, the easier it will be to reach your goals.

By starting to save early, you are able to take control of your future. I'm sure you can imagine the people you know who aren't in control of their finances. Start saving now, and you'll be well on your way to avoiding those dangers.

Even if you can only save one or two hundred dollars a month, you are teaching yourself self-control and discipline.

Most of us have heard the parable of the talents. A rich man went on a journey and entrusted his servants with his property while he was away. He gave five talents to one servant, two to another, and one to the last servant.

The servants with five and two talents traded and bartered with their talents and each doubled them. But the servant with one, buried his in the ground until the master returned.

When the master returned, he was pleased with the servants who had doubled their talents, but to the one who buried his in the ground he yelled, "You wicked, lazy servant! You ought to have invested my money with the bankers, and at my coming I should have received what was my own with interest."

If they knew the importance of interest and saving 2,000 years ago, we might want to take note.

Overspending your money can destroy your life. I've seen it rip apart marriages and families.

But I don't think it needs to be that way. You can control your finances, you can save early, and you will benefit in the future. Don't allow yourself to be controlled by what culture suggests you want or need.

Take control of your future and start investing your money now

LESSON Nº. SEVEN:
Believe You Can.

Whatever the mind of man can conceive and believe, it can achieve. —*Napoleon Hill*

We're so quick to doubt ourselves. We doubt because it's easier than believing. Believing takes having faith in something you can't see.

In the circus, elephants are trained from a young age to wear chains around one leg so they can't wander away. While an elephant is young, he fights the chains, wandering as far as he can and pulling the chains tight. Over time, the elephant stops trying, knowing he can't escape the chain. But as he grows, the chains become weaker and the elephant, stronger.

There comes a time when the elephant could easily break the chain. But because the elephant has believed for so long it can't, in the end, it doesn't. It doesn't matter that the adult elephant is 100 times stronger than the chain holding him; all that matters is whether he believes the chain is stronger.

So often we allow ourselves to be chained in the exact same way.

Early in my life and career, I lacked confidence. To be honest, I still struggle with that now as an accomplished entrepreneur. When I was younger, I believed there were a lot of things I couldn't do. I missed a lot of opportunities because I chose to believe I couldn't take them and succeed. Sometimes I would focus so much on all the things that could go wrong they eventually did. As I focused on problems rather than solutions, failure became a self-fulfilling prophesy.

On the other hand, when you begin to believe in yourself, you allow yourself to try and take risks. The more you try, the more you succeed. And the more times you succeed with small things, the more you will believe in yourself to take on bigger ideas and dreams. The more you can see something, the easier it is to believe it's possible.

Science has proven that people who don't believe they can succeed are much less likely to succeed, while people who believe they can are much more willing to do what it takes to reach their goal. **Always believe you can.**

LESSON N°. EIGHT:

Have a Passion to Inspire.

If your actions inspire others to dream more, learn more, do more and become more, you are a leader.

—John Quincy Adams

Merriam Webster Dictionary defines passion as, "A strong feeling of enthusiasm or excitement for something." On the other hand, the second definition is, "a strong feeling (such as *anger*) that causes you to act in a dangerous way."

Passion is the feeling that rises when your favorite team wins the championship. It's the anger you feel about the injustice of human trafficking, that buzz in your ear saying *you need to do something*.

But passion is also what produces and leads to terrorist attacks.

You see, passion is often viewed as a great, positive emotion but it can actually be positive or negative. You must first recognize however it is used, passion is powerful.

What is that for you? What is the thing you can't stop thinking about? Is there something you want to see happen so badly you'd be willing to risk everything?

Find that and go after it.

The passion you have can greatly influence the people around you. Have you ever talked with someone who had this kind of passion? You walk away from the conversation inspired. Something in you is different.

What if you could leave that kind of impact on someone else's life? **How do you want to inspire them?**

I remember the first time I heard the story behind Toms shoes. That's the story of a guy who saw a need, had a passion, and followed it. He has now given over a million pairs of shoes to children in need around the world—all because he followed his passion.

His story changed my perspective on life and inspired me to find my own passion. So I founded a company that combined my passion for developing and equipping leaders with my love of baseball. Even in the company's early stages, I have now seen others inspired by our willingness to find and pursue our passion while helping others.

Over the years, I've found this is the most

fulfilling way to use my passion: not only to accomplish my own dreams, but to inspire others to pursue their passions, too.

Find your passion and pursue it wholeheartedly, and as you do you'll empower others to do the same.

LESSON N°. NINE:
Be Decisive.

In any moment of decision, the best thing you can do is the right thing. The worst thing you can do is nothing. —Theodore Roosevelt

Twenty years ago I owned a travel company. In the beginning stages of forming the company we looked to hire someone for outside sales. I had a friend who I thought would be a perfect fit for the job, so I asked her to interview for the position. I was sure I was going to hire her, and throughout the interview, I led her to believe she was the exact person I was looking for.

But when I went home that night, I started having second thoughts, debating whether or not she was really right for the job. I went back and forth for days and put off talking to her even longer. I couldn't decide. In the end, through my indecision, not only did I lose a person who could have been valuable to the business, but I greatly damaged our relationship in the process.

Because I was afraid of making the wrong decision, I made no decision, and it was my indecision that ended up hurting me the most.

Have you ever experienced that paralyzing fear while you're making a decision? It seems like the decision in front of you will change your life. Sometimes it even feels like you're just one bad decision away from losing everything.

That's a terrifying feeling, but it's never really the case. Losing everything takes bad decision after bad decision for years.

It's okay to be afraid to make decisions, but don't let that fear stop you from deciding. Even if you make the wrong decision, there will always be ways to fix it or make another decision to change directions.

Commitment is hard, but the consequences of not making a decision are worse. When you put off making decisions, you miss out on incredible opportunities. And on a more practical note, the longer you wait to do things, the more expensive things generally are.

I'm not saying you should flip a coin to make your decisions. It's incredibly important to learn to be discerning and seek the advice of mentors. When you understand your values you have a guiding light that gives you the confidence to make decisions. But at the end of the day, you need to muster up your courage and make a decision.

The good news is, this gets easier with practice. Decisiveness breeds confidence: the more decisions you make, the more confident you will be in your ability to make decisions.

Being decisive is a major key to success because your decisions can be extremely powerful.

Decide what you want to do and do it.

LESSON Nº. TEN:
Live Your Dream.

*The biggest adventure you can take is to live the
life of your dreams. —Oprah Winfrey*

Dreaming unlocks your full potential, helping you see how you can take the impossible and make it possible. To begin dreaming you need to ask yourself...

What would you do if you could do anything?

Dreaming great dreams is essential—but it's only the first step. Many people have dreams, but few turn them into reality. You must learn to live your dreams in a world all too ready to give you reasons not to.

Sometimes your dreams are going to seem crazy, but I dare you to pursue them anyway. Don't let the fact that it seems too hard or too big stop you from trying. Don't let your doubts or fears hold you back from pursuing those dreams.

There will be times when you will be tempted to abandon your dreams, tempted not to pursue them or live them out. You will be tempted to settle; to accept that where you are is good enough. And if you settle for too long, you'll begin to believe your dreams aren't worth pursuing and miss out on abundant living.

But settling to dream without acting is like taxiing around a runway in an airplane without ever taking off. The plane will get you around, but it's not made to stay on the runway—and neither are your dreams.

The truth is, your dreams are worth pursuing. They aren't random coincidence or silly thoughts: you were made to accomplish great things.

I've seen too many friends settle for less than their full potential and regret it later. There are times I've wanted to settle, and even times when I have settled. There have been dreams I've wanted to pursue but never did. There have also been times I have pursued a dream and failed.

But in the end, my greatest regrets are the times I didn't try. Those regrets always cut deeper than the times I tried and failed.

Living your dream is a scary risk, but it's far more rewarding than settling. You have the wide-open opportunity to decide who you you want to be and what you want to do. So take a risk, choose not to settle, and live your dream.

There will come a time when you will ask

yourself once again:

What would you do if you could do anything?

And you will answer, "Exactly what I am doing now."

Then you will know you are living your dream. This answer is possible!

Pursue your dreams until it's true for you.

LESSON Nº. ELEVEN:

Embrace the Potential, Not the Flaws.

When you look for the good in others, you discover the best in yourself.

I've mentored a lot of young men and developed many great relationships. But although I wish I could say it's always worked out perfectly, it hasn't.

I once encountered a young man who used and dealt drugs and was destroying his family in the process. Honestly, I didn't want to reach out or try to help. But my wife Robin insisted, reminding me, "We need to look for the potential in him." So I began to mentor him, and for a period of time, he even lived with our family.

Throughout the next year, our lives were transformed. As we mentored him and welcomed him into our home and family, we saw a radical change in his life. Not only did this change affect his family, but it affected ours.

Sadly, he eventually fell back into his drug addiction, and just a few weeks ago, he passed away from an overdose. It was some of the saddest news I have ever received.

In the wake of his death I was reminded how glad I was that I had invested in him. Regardless of the final outcome, I was able to see the best in him and it changed a lot of others' lives in the process.

Working with people is always going to be messy. Sometimes you're going to get hurt and sometimes you're going to hurt someone else. Because you've been hurt, you'll be tempted to believe the worst about people. Don't.

When you believe in others, they'll begin to believe in themselves. And when you look for the best in someone, they'll look for it in themselves.

When you shift your focus to the positive things someone has to offer, you give them the opportunity to make a change in their life. Investing in that young man was one of the most rewarding things I've ever done. I saw his attitude and outlook on life completely change when he realized someone saw him for more than just his flaws and the mistakes he had made.

Working with people will often be hard, but everyone has something to offer. If you look for the best in everyone, you'll be more effective, and change others' lives along the way.

Seek to inspire and encourage those around you, and always look for the best in everyone.

LESSON Nº. TWELVE:
Have Fun.

Just Play. Have Fun. Enjoy the game.
—Michael Jordan

Imagine this:

Your eyes sting as you stare at your computer screen. You glance at the stack of paperwork to your right and sigh. The only light illuminating your corner office is the glow of your desk lamp; the sun set hours ago and everyone else left long before that. You begin to wonder, *When did I become so consumed with work?*

It's so easy to get caught up in our work and the serious things we need to do as responsible adults. But that life becomes draining and can even feel meaningless.

If you don't set apart time to have fun in the midst of the mundane, you won't make it. Plan trips, invite people over, and go on adventures just to have fun. Make a commitment to having fun. See your best friends and make time for your hobbies and passions. You need to set this time apart to embrace and enjoy life; to celebrate life's adventure.

Sometimes, though, you don't have time to plan fun, and you just have to choose to have fun. In the midst of apparent chaos you should always choose to have fun. I remember rainy weekends with my sons, sliding down the huge mountains of dirt and playing in the mud. We had food fights in the backyard because sometimes you just have to clean out the refrigerator. Dr. Seuss said it very simply, "Fun is good!"

Have you ever had a really terrible day? Of course, we all do. On those days, when I need to be reminded of what's important in life, I like to go to a playground or a ballpark and watch children play. You can learn a lot about fun and life from 5 year olds. Children play because they enjoy it. They don't play to impress people or to get a promotion. They are enjoying the present and are fully engaged in life.

Learn to see chaos and the mundane as opportunities for fun. When you're stuck in traffic, jam out and talk with your friends. When you get hard news, take the opportunity to dream. When you have car troubles, learn from them. Choose to have fun in the midst of apparent chaos.

The older you get, the faster life goes by. So have fun, embrace the moments that seem like disasters—and laugh. And go to the playground every now and then!

LESSON N°. THIRTEEN:
Be a Little Crazy.

If being crazy means living life as if it matters, then I don't mind being completely insane. —Kate Winslet

A few years ago my oldest son and I signed up for a half marathon just a few weeks before the race. We hadn't trained at all and were not in the best of shape, but we thought it would be fun to try. People told us we were crazy to think we could just sign up and run. But we did it anyways. We finished the half marathon and it was an incredible experience.

I remember crossing the finish line thinking two things: *This is incredible. How did I pull this off?*

In order to experience that feeling, I had to do something that seemed crazy to other people.

Being "crazy" means you're taking risks and trying things that have never been done before. I firmly believe if you've never had anyone tell you,

"You're CRAZY," you're missing something.

On the way to achieving your dreams, you'll have to take some risks. Those risks might look big and scary, and other people might call you crazy for taking them. And with any risk you take, it's always possible you'll fail. But imagine if every person who was told they were crazy listened and stopped what they were doing. The world would be a completely different place: we most likely wouldn't have computers, airplanes, or Instagram.

My good friend Jeremie moved to Russia right after he graduated college to start a business. Many people called him crazy and he may have been. But this experience was a defining time in his entrepreneurial life. He was just being a pioneer finding out who he was.

I'm not telling you to jump out of an airplane without a parachute. It is possible to be too crazy, and so it's important to surround yourself with mentors you trust who can help you learn to make wise decisions. But it's important to be a little crazy. I've started businesses, taken risky trips, become a pilot and even decided to write a book—all decisions other people have called crazy. Through those "crazy" ventures not only have I had the most fun, but I have seen possibilities for greatness I would otherwise have missed.

Not taking the safe route will always seem a little crazy, but who wants to stay safe? **Nothing**

exciting happens on the sidelines. Sure you're safe and comfortable, but greatness isn't found there. I've found by taking these risks, you learn you are capable of more than you could ever imagine.

Don't be daunted when someone calls your great idea "crazy": get out there and take the risk.

LESSON N°. FOURTEEN:
Share Your Feelings.

The best and most beautiful things in the world cannot be seen or even touched. They must be felt with the heart. —Helen Keller

Feelings are often perceived as weakness. Our society doesn't talk about them very much and instead we focus more on our actions. We talk about what we're doing over the weekend, how work is going, and what we think about the economy.

The problem with not sharing your feelings is you develop shallow friendships and over time will find you are never really known or understood by those around you.

If you aren't honest and don't share your feelings, you will never develop authentic relationships.

In 2008 I was experiencing severe financial problems from some failed businesses and failed investments. It came to a point where even getting out of bed was hard. I was stressed and depressed.

On Sunday I went to church and saw all of my normal friends. We talked about sports and what we had done that weekend. A friend turned to me and asked, "So, how are you doing?"

"Can I *really* tell you?" I asked him. And as we talked about what was really going on, I shared how much I was hurting and having a hard time coping.

This changed my life.

Our conversation led to an even more honest friendship, and the support of others in our friend circle. This support that I received from sharing openly with these friends helped pull me out of depression. Over the years as these friends have gone through hard times, they've been able to share their experiences of pain, addiction, and broken relationships. Through vulnerably sharing our deepest hurts, we have found how much stronger we are together. Our relationships have deepened as we've helped one another through difficult times.

Sharing real feelings is always a risk. You have to risk to trust someone else, but it's always worth it. My life changed when I chose to be honest about the hard times I was going through.

It is impossible to make it through life without authentic relationships. But these relationships don't just happen; you have to take the risk to share how you feel.

You might think your feelings make you appear weak, but sharing your feelings is essential to building friendships that will get you through life's ups and downs.

LESSON N°. FIFTEEN:
Less Talk. More Action.

Walk the walk... talk ain't necessary.
—*George Akoma Jr.*

We've all met someone who speaks flawlessly, tells incredible stories, and can make you believe almost anything. These people know all the right words and have an incredible gift to cast vision.

The interesting thing I've learned over the years about these people is their words don't always equal their actions.

A lot of people say things they don't really mean, and you need to be aware of that.

About ten years ago, I entered a partnership with someone recommended to me by a friend. He had an incredible resume, was very well spoken, and cast a great vision for the company, describing to us all he had done in the past and all he planned to do for our company. His enthusiasm sold me. I forgot to look closely at his actual track record.

A few months went by, but although he was still excited, not much action was happening. The promises he had been making weren't materializing. A few more months went by and the same thing was happening.

When I stopped to look a little closer, it was obvious he was all talk. He hadn't done as much in the past and it didn't look like he was going to do much in the future besides talk about his ideas.

A lot of people are polished and can tell a good story, but people's actions, past and present, are a much better indicator of who they are.

Let's say you know two people who want to lose weight and get in shape. The first person tells you how excited they are to lose weight and they talk about how great it will be when they're thinner. They tell you the plans they have for their diet and the gyms they're thinking about joining.

The second person might tell you they want to lose weight, but they also tell you they signed up at the gym last weekend. You see them carve out time to go to the gym. You also see the lunch they bring to work is healthier.

Who are you more likely to believe?

It's important to be able to recognize the people who are all talk, but it is even more important not to be one of those people.

As a dreamer, it's sometimes hard for me

to not be that person. I have a lot of ideas and dreams. I love to tell people my vision for an idea, but it often looks like I'm not following through. This leads to a lack of credibility and reliability. In these situations it's important to qualify when you're dreaming, not promising.

Promises are easy to make, but not as easy to keep. Always remember to watch what people do, not just what they say they'll do. **Make sure your actions always align with your words.**

LESSON Nº. SIXTEEN:
Turn Off the Faucet.

Insanity is doing the same thing over and over and expecting a different result. —Albert Einstein

Back when I ran a travel agency, I had a consultant, Don, tell me, "Stop sweeping all the water off the floor and turn off the faucet."

When you see a bunch of water on the floor, the first thing you want to do is to clean it up. But if you don't look for the source and find where the water came from, you'll be constantly cleaning up water for years.

He wasn't referring to a pipe, but rather my good intentions of trying to fix the symptoms of bigger problems in many areas of my life.

Life is messy and sometimes there are going to be leaks.

I used to own an office building in Atlanta that was a constant challenge. We continually had moisture problems and even had water from upper levels coming through the ceiling. I tried to alleviate the issue, and patched and painted the ceilings several times.

But a few years into the problem, we had to do a major renovation of the entire ground floor. We also had to call in a specialist to remediate the mold. All because I ignored the root problem. It was an expensive reminder of the lesson Don had taught me twenty years earlier.

When we ignore or don't look for the real problem behind the symptoms, the consequences only get worse. The lesson applies to every area of life, from plumbing to business to relationships. More often than not, if you're consistently having problems or fights with someone, there is a bigger problem that needs to be solved.

Problems, leaks, and fights are part of life. You have to recognize that, or you'll end up ignoring these things and the problems will only get bigger and harder to solve. Ask yourself, "Am I solving the bigger problem? Or am I just curing the symptoms?"

Even so, you might not even realize you've been tending to the symptoms without solving the root. One way to determine this is to ask yourself if this is a repetitive problem. Are you patching holes every few months? Are you fighting about the same thing every other week?

It is easy to get so caught up with cleaning up the mess in front of you that you forget about the bigger problem, but the temporary solution is never worth its long-term price. I've seen relationships destroyed and costly repairs needed to be made. I want you to avoid these hardships as best you can.

Find the root of the problem, don't just cure the symptoms.

LESSON Nº. SEVENTEEN:
Create a Good Name.

A good name is to be chosen over great riches.
—*King Solomon*

As an entrepreneur, I have been a part of many successful companies and others that have failed miserably. When the economy crashed in 2008, I went through some hard times and many of my companies went out of business.

In the midst of the chaos, my companies had bank loans and bills we couldn't pay and partners who lost money.

Throughout the turmoil, I was extremely open with banks, partners, clients, and vendors. I tried to handle the situation by doing the right thing and being honest with everyone. I was proactive at a time when most people were being reactive.

Over the years, I was able to work out and make good on my loans, while a lot of other businesses and people couldn't. Because I was open and honest about what was going on, the bankers and partners saw I could be trusted even in difficult times.

As a result, I now have bankers who will lend to me, vendors who will extend credit, and partners who will invest with me despite the past failures. All because I created a good name and trusting relationships throughout the years.

Proverbs 22:1 reads, "A good name is to be chosen over great riches." Don't sacrifice your reputation for money. Who you are is so much more important than what you do and how much you may accumulate.

A good name takes years to build and only moments to destroy. When faced with a decision, don't just choose what's potentially *profitable*—choose what's *right*.

LESSON Nº. EIGHTEEN:
Work is an Experience.

*Choose who your work **for**, rather than what you **do**, especially early in your career.*

Finding a job can be hard. Especially after college, the pressure to choose a career and begin to pay off student loans can be overwhelming.

When my friend Ray graduated from Georgia Tech, he felt this pressure. He interviewed with a dozen companies and was offered several jobs. The lowest-paying offer came from a man named Mr. Moye. Ray reluctantly chose this job despite the low salary. In the years that followed, Mr. Moye invested in Ray both personally and professionally. Because Ray took this job, he was trained more carefully in all aspects of the business and learned more than he ever would have at a larger, higher paying business.

Now Ray runs a highly successful company, in part because of the training and investment he received from Mr. Moye.

This story isn't an anomaly. I know dozens of these stories, and honestly, behind most successful CEOs and companies are stories like these. The best way to learn the business is to work closely with someone who is already doing it. You'll avoid a lot of mistakes and learn a lot of the shortcuts that way.

I heard a story of a writer recently who worked with a CEO of a large non-profit at a significantly lower price than she normally would. She emphasized how "worth it" it was to create that relationship and learn from him.

Early on in your career it is especially important to be careful about who you work for, rather than how much you make. The experience and potential relationships you will create will shape your future career and further it more than accepting a higher paying job with less experience.

The value that is found in relationships that can guide and mentor you in your early years will shape your life and future far more than any salary ever could.

LESSON Nº. NINETEEN:
Solve Problems Creatively.

Creativity can solve almost any problem. The creative act, the defeat of habit by originality, overcomes everything. —George Lois

A problem is defined as, "a matter or situation regarded as unwelcome or harmful and needing to be dealt with and overcome."

We're good at identifying problems. We can be quick to recognize something isn't right or could be improved.

In the dozens of businesses I've helped lead, problems run rampant and that is to be expected. The value in a leader is not identifying the problem, but actually solving it.

The most successful businesses are those that find creative new solutions to problems.

Uber exemplifies this mindset. The company identified a problem: people are drinking and driving. Then they designed a new solution: get someone else to drive them. They created an app that enables users to request a ride from anywhere, at any time, to get almost any place.

As a result, the cities where Uber is used most have actually seen a decline in drunk driving arrests and accidents

The creators of Uber didn't just identify a problem—they found a new way to solve it that is making a difference in the world.

People who creatively solve problems are much more valuable to a company or organization. **Being a creative problem solver will open doors and create more opportunities than you ever imagined.**

Being a problem solver isn't easy; it takes creativity and tenacity. But this life skill will take you to the next level and make you extremely valuable to your employers. Not only will you see a new way of doing things, but in the process you will discover the value of thinking outside the box.

Instead of complaining about a problem, try solving it.

LESSON Nº. TWENTY:
The Questions You Ask Matter.

He who knows all the answers has not been asked all the questions. —Confucius

Throughout my years of dealing with customers, employees, and business ventures, I've realized most people don't know what they want. I've held meetings with customers about particular products and realized halfway through they wanted something completely different. There's often so much going on in a person that you can discover with good questions.

The best way to figure out what's going on behind the scenes is to **ask**.

Our perceptions about what the other person sees might be wrong.

It's similar to an optical illusion. There's a popular drawing showing two different images depending on how you look at it. Some people look at the drawing and see the face of an old woman. Others look at it and see a young girl with her head turned. Imagine trying to talk to someone about this picture when you each see different things. Neither one of you is wrong, but your perspective is different.

The only way to see other perspectives and find out what is going on in the mind of the other person is to **ask questions**.

Asking questions also means we need to listen to others' answers. Listen twice as much as you speak because by talking too much you can never really hear what the other person is saying or find out what is important to them.

As you ask good questions and listen to the answers, you will form deeper connections and understand the motivations and desires of others. To form meaningful relationships you should always remember to be interested before being interesting.

The ability to ask good questions is a skill that will set you apart. Asking good questions and listening will change your life. The questions you ask matter, so choose them carefully.

LESSON Nº. TWENTY-ONE:
Servant Leadership.

There is but one just use of power, and it is to serve people. —*George H.W. Bush*

I've held leadership roles of various capacities pretty much constantly for the last thirty years. When you've spent that much time leading others, you learn a lot about what works—and what doesn't.

When I first began to lead others, I thought leadership was about authority. I thought leadership meant managing others and telling people what to do. My mistake is a common misconception; many leaders try to lead through the weight of their position, saying things like, "Well, I'm your boss, so you'll do what I say."

But position-based leadership creates animosity. It produces no trust or loyalty, and when hard times come, the people who are "following" won't stick around for long—sailors mutiny against their captain and workers go on strike.

Never try to lead simply from a position of authority. When you lead like that, you have no true influence, and if you don't have influence among your people, you won't last long as a leader.

A good leader doesn't just tell people what to do: they have influence with the people they're leading. A good leader has followers who want to follow them.

So how do you gain influence? Jesus shifted the paradigm of leadership from something based on position to something based on servanthood.

When a leader is humble and shows their people they really care about them, the people grow to trust their leader, and this trust generates loyalty. As the people's trust gradually builds, the leader gains the kind of influence that can impact nations.

Jesus said, "For I come not to be served but to serve." And more radically said, "If anyone would be first, he must be last of all, and servant to all." **Leadership is about influence.** When you follow Jesus' example, you can lead from the board room or the mailroom—no title needed.

Demonstrate to those around you that you care about them, not just the task they're working on. Those who serve others will gain influence enough to change the world. These are the leaders who are worth following.

Be one of these leaders.

LESSON Nᵒ. TWENTY-TWO:
Empower Dreams.

It's a thrill to fulfill your own childhood dreams, but as you get older, you may find that enabling the dreams of others is even more fun. —Randy Pausch

We all have dreams. Some people dream of starting successful companies; others dream of traveling to foreign countries. In your own life, you've probably experienced the power of having someone who comes alongside you to support you as you pursue your dreams. Sometimes support means the difference between wishful thinking and making your dreams a reality.

You can be that person for others. **Look for ways to enable the dreams of the people around you.**

Truett Cathy, founder of Chick-fil-A, is one of my heroes in how he embraced this concept. While building the company, he made it a company value to enable people's dreams of owning a business. He made franchisement more accessible to those who really wanted and dreamed of owning a business. By enabling the dreams of others, he built a tremendously successful company full of employees and operators who are fiercely loyal to the company and Truett personally. Although not intended to be a self-serving strategy, there is no doubt by enabling others he helped guarantee the success of his company.

You don't have to own a billion-dollar company to help others accomplish their dreams; there are lots of small but meaningful ways you can move them forward. I've done this many times, often without even realizing it. Sometimes it's as simple as an introduction or helping someone make a connection.

It's not as much about what you physically do for someone, but by having a spirit of helpfulness and optimism.

Even when you feel like you have nothing to offer, you have the ability to impact others and help them follow their dreams. Your voice is powerful—often it just takes one person reminding someone their dream is valid and possible to keep them going.

In a world full of doubters, be the voice saying, *"You can."*

One of the greatest joys in life is enabling the dreams of others. When I look back and see how many people's dreams I've even been a small part of, I realize how rewarding this process is.

Always choose to be part of helping enable someone's dream.

LESSON Nº. TWENTY-THREE:
Never Give Up.

It is hard to beat a person who never gives up.
—*Babe Ruth*

One of my good friends, Jeff Shinabarger, has a mantra: "No one said changing the world was going to be easy!"

As an entrepreneur, I've wanted to give up hundreds of times. Often in the moment, when I felt stressed and overwhelmed, giving up seemed like the only option. Sometimes I've caved and thrown in the towel.

But other times, I've chosen to persevere, even when a situation seemed impossible. In the end, the times I persevered were some of my most successful endeavors.

Bernie Marcus, the founder of Home Depot, once told me the story of how he started the company. He was turned down by 30 or 40 bankers when he was looking for a loan to start Home Depot. He told me in the face of overwhelming rejection and opposition, he continually had to choose to believe in his dream and idea.

After months of struggle and disappointment, he finally found a bank that took a chance on him—and the rest is history.

This may seem extreme, but in reality it's not. Almost every successful company has a story similar to this. So don't be surprised when you come up against these hard situations and want to give up. Remember success belongs to those who persevere.

This principle applies to more than just business: perseverance will lead to success in every part of your life. It can apply to your athletic pursuits or your dream of being elected president.

There are two areas, though, where perseverance is especially important.

1. Relationships. Don't give up on relationships. Of course there are times relationships need to end, but that's not the same as giving up. Pursue the best for one another relentlessly. The best things in life require you to fight relentlessly.

2. Yourself. Most importantly, don't give up on yourself. You probably don't realize the amount of times you've given up on yourself. All the times you thought you couldn't do something, every time you turned back because you believed you weren't good enough or smart enough, you gave up on yourself.

But you have an endless amount of potential, so don't give up on yourself. Always believe you can be better and grow. It's not about winning, it's about pursuing the things you once perceived as impossible. As Winston Churchill said, "never, never, never give up."

There will always be problems that seem insurmountable. So when you want to give up, I dare you to persevere. Everyone faces hardships. The most successful people are the ones who don't give up, no matter what.

It's easy to quit and most people do, but success comes to those who **never give up**.

LESSON N°. TWENTY-FOUR:
People Over Things.

Love people and use things, not the other way around.

Imagine this with me:

You just bought a brand new convertible. You've wanted this car for years and now you finally have it. You drive to your sister's house and your nephews hop in the back of the car, their eyes wide in excitement over the "cool" new car. Their mother warns them, "Be careful not to mess up the new car!"

You take the kids for a drive to get ice cream. As you return home and pull into the driveway, one of the boys drops his chocolate ice cream cone on your white leather seats. The boy looks up at you teary eyed, knowing his mistake was costly.

My first reaction would have been to yell and clean up the mess immediately. But what would happen if I slowed down enough to assess what was truly most important?

What would you do?

People and relationships are so much more important than any possessions. At the end of your life, as you're taking your last breaths, you won't be asking your family to show you a picture of your car or your phone or your new gadgets, you'll want to see those close to you.

A few years ago a young man I mentored was invited to a wedding. He told me he didn't have a suit, so I invited him over to look in my closet for something that might work for him. At first I thought I would offer him one of my old suits, but I watched and let him pick out one of my best suits and try it on. He looked in the mirror, a smile lit up his face and he stood higher and more confident than I had ever seen him before.

When I saw the look on his face, my life was changed. The impact this gesture made on him was so much more valuable than the suit itself. In this moment I thought, "How could I ever value things over people?" The outcome of putting someone else before my possessions was far more valuable than anything I could have owned.

Is it more important to jump when your iPhone signals a text or to focus on the friend sharing a story with you over dinner?

Things break, fade away, and are even replaced. Relationships last a lifetime.

Learn to value people over things and you will change the lives of others as well as your own life.

LESSON Nº. TWENTY-FIVE:
Always Learn.

Live as if you were to die tomorrow. Learn as if you were to live forever. —*Mahatma Gandhi*

At 47-years-old, I entered a year long leadership training program called X-Core through Giant Worldwide. Before this program I had been to hundreds of presentations and conferences on leadership and self-improvement. I have a degree in business and have owned dozens of businesses. However, the most growth I have ever experienced has occurred within the two years since joining that program. Why? Because I adopted the mindset to see every opportunity as a learning experience.

Some people are born with a hunger for knowledge, and others develop the hunger over time. But all of these people are lifelong learners and will be more successful because of it.

When you embrace learning, you open yourself up to opportunities for growth and improvement. You'll find new ways of running your business or helping the marginalized because your mind is open to learning about the possibilities around you.

You also need to see each day as an opportunity to learn something new. This is how you integrate learning into your everyday life. Did you get a flat tire? See it as an opportunity to learn how to change the tire. Hungry? See it as an opportunity to learn to cook something new. Need to go somewhere new? See it as an opportunity to learn about different places. This is how you become a lifelong learner: adopt the mindset into everything you do.

How does this look practically?

Have a list of books to read instead of watching TV or scrolling social media. Try listening to podcasts instead of music in your car every once in awhile.

Once you hear about something new, don't just listen to how great or interesting this new thing or concept is. Try it. If you listen to a podcast about overcoming fear, why not try it? If you read a book about minimalism, why not try it?

We live in the age of information. You can Google how to do almost anything. Want to learn to build a website? Do it. Want to learn to cook? Ask your friends to join a culinary class.

According to *Entrepreneur Online*, "there is a direct correlation between individuals who strive for growth in their personal lives and those who thrive in their professional lives."

The most successful people in life are those who are always willing to learn more. Embracing the "learn always" mindset opens you up to new business ventures and tools that could improve your success. Life is always more fulfilling when you're learning and trying new things.

LESSON N°. TWENTY-SIX:
4:8 Principle.

Whatever is pure, noble, lovely and excellent—
think about such things. —Paul

When you're in the trenches of life, you can get stuck focusing on what's going wrong around you. The chaos of life needs your attention, but if you're not careful, the chaos will consume you.

There was a time in my life when I was depressed and struggled to get out of bed. I couldn't see a silver lining and felt like everything was falling apart.

One day a friend came over and introduced me to the 4:8 principle.

This idea comes from Tommy Newberry's book *The 4:8 Principle*. The principle is based off of Philippians 4:8.

"Finally, brothers and sisters, whatever is true, whatever is noble, whatever is right, whatever is pure, whatever is lovely, whatever is admirable—if anything is excellent or praiseworthy—think about such things." —

Philippians 4:8

I had been focusing on everything that was going wrong for so long I eventually believed my life was falling apart. It's a dangerous path to get stuck on.

My friend told me to write a list of all the things I was thankful for. Hesitantly, I wrote the list, and as I wrote it, my perspective shifted and my life was changed.

When I brought attention to everything I was thankful for and everything that was going well, I was able to break the negative focus and realized my life wasn't falling apart. I was amazed by the number of things I was thankful for.

As I wrote, I found purpose again. I saw the names of my family and friends on the list and was reminded in the midst of these difficult circumstances, I still had them.

Most likely setting your mind on the good things in your life will remind you of people. And that will remind you of your purpose.

Setting your mind on these things will change your life. There is always more than you think there is to be thankful for.

So be grateful, and remember how changing your perspective can change your life.

LESSON N⁰. TWENTY-SEVEN:

Don't Worry About the Popular People.

Popularity is the greatest lie in the world.
—*Thomas Carlyle*

Whether or not we like to admit it, popularity is a driving force in how we operate in society. In high school, college, and sometimes even in the workplace, most kids, and adults as well, want to be part of the popular crowd. In school the pursuit of popularity feels like one of the most important things in the world.

I've seen countless times how often people get hurt in the pursuit of trying to be accepted by this popular crowd. Even more, I've seen how quickly the "popular" crowd can change and how one wrong move can ruin your "popularity."

The problem with popular relationships is they are generally **superficial**. They're often based largely on partying or outer appearance and lack real substance.

So at the end of the day, don't worry about the popular people. Instead of pursuing popularity, pursue authentic relationships.

I mentored a young man a few years ago who struggled with feeling accepted by the popular crowd. He constantly felt like he was an outsider in high school and lacked confidence because of that. As he grew and graduated high school, he began to look for authentic friendships and he found them. As he began to create meaningful relationships, he began to thrive. Now, by finding these friendships, he has become confident and secure in his identity with friends who push him to be even better.

Being popular is okay. It's great being liked and looked up to if you are emulating worthy characteristics. I hope you will strive to stand up for the "unpopular" person rather than striving to be accepted by the "popular."

And remember popularity is fickle; in the end it means nothing. So don't put much stock in what "popular" people say about you. (They're just trying to make themselves feel better.)

At the end of the day, always strive to create deep, meaningful relationships. When you are authentic and look for meaningful relationships you will find them. And these relationships will mean more than any popularity you could have ever achieved. Choose authenticity over being cool every time.

LESSON Nº. TWENTY-EIGHT:
Choosing Friends.

As iron sharpens iron, so a friend sharpens a
friend. —Ancient Proverb

As much as I sometimes wish I could, I can't do life alone. Neither can you. **Life is meant to be shared.**

Throughout my life I've seen how necessary friendships are, especially in difficult times. In my neighborhood, there have been a number of tragic deaths my sons had to deal with. Every time their friends' outpouring of support has been inspiring and uplifting to see. They would have struggled to make it through some hard times without those friends.

Meaningful relationships with others are vital to getting through—and enjoying—life's ups and downs.

Because friends are so important, deciding who they are is just as important as having them.

One of my favorite things about friends is that

you really get to choose them. Choosing friends in childhood is the first major decision a person gets to make. This decision of who our ongoing, lifelong friends are is also one of the most defining decisions we make throughout our lives.

Why? Because the people you surround yourself with will have the greatest impact on your day-to-day life.

It's scientifically proven that our friends influence not only the decisions we make, but who we actually become over time. What your mother always said is true: Bad company corrupts good character. And, hanging out with the wrong people will never help you do the right thing.

A few years ago, I was in a business partnership with someone who didn't share any of my values. But because we were working so closely on a project, I found myself around him constantly and having to talk to him almost daily. I remember the first time I conceded in a decision I didn't want to make. I knew the choice would compromise my values, but with him next to me urging me to agree, I agreed. Over the next few months I slowly found myself making more decisions that brought me further away from who I wanted to be.

When someone influences you, it is always a slow fade that gradually changes you over time.

I eventually stopped and looked back over the decisions I had been making and realized I was way off course. I had never wanted to be in a place like this, but because I surrounded myself with someone who didn't hold or respect my values, I found myself compromised. It almost destroyed my business and the reputation I had built as a businessman with integrity.

I made the hard decision to leave the partnership. It was difficult in the moment, but ultimately one of the best decisions of my life.

The people you spend large amounts of time with will influence you in ways you might not even be aware of, and over time, bad friends can have a major negative impact on your life.

On the other hand, friends who share your value system can have a profound positive effect on your life, encouraging you to be even better.

I've seen the power of positive friendships change the trajectory of someone's life. Having friends who believe in you is proven to improve your self-confidence. I have seen the positive impact of friends encouraging each other to pursue their dreams, overcome addiction, and persevere through life's challenges.

The people you associate with can radically change your life positively or negatively. Are you choosing friends who build you up or bring you down?

Be aware of who you associate with, not only to protect your reputation but to guard your heart and character. Choose to surround yourself with people who believe in you and will tell you the hard things.

LESSON Nº. TWENTY-NINE:
Try New Things.

The more you read the more things you will know.
The more you learn the more places you will go.

—*Dr. Seuss*

Doing new things is hard. It's why a lot of kids don't like trying new foods. Sticking to what you know is easy and comfortable. But if you always stay inside your comfort zone you'll end up with a lot of regrets.

A friend of mine just went to Europe for the first time. At the beginning of the trip she thought she had a pretty good idea of how things would work. She arrived one morning at a friend's house in the Netherlands and was offered breakfast: a piece of bread with peanut butter and chocolate sprinkles on it. She laughed, but found herself with a new favorite breakfast food. She realized maybe life might be even better when she gave new, different things a chance.

Embracing diversity starts with realizing

that sometimes things are just different, but that doesn't make those things wrong or bad. Let's be honest—having chocolate sprinkles for breakfast is definitely an improvement to our lives.

From the Netherlands, she traveled to Greece. After finding that trying new foods can be an incredible experience, she went to a coffee shop near her hostel in Greece, and decided she had to try the "Greek Coffee" they offered. She took one sip and hated it. She described it as tasting "strangely like dirt."

That's the truth about embracing diversity: sometimes, you'll drink a cup of dirt and hate it. But without tasting the bad cups of coffee, you might never find the one you've been waiting for.

This doesn't just apply to food. You need to embrace diversity in every part of your life. One of my biggest regrets from college is that I didn't take diverse classes. Even the electives I chose were related to my major, Business Administration. But if I could go back, I'd make myself take a pottery or poetry class. Perhaps I could be the next Edgar Allan Poe who never tried to write a poem. (I'm probably not, but you don't know if you don't try.)

Make friends with different backgrounds. Take a dance class. Order something other than your "regular." Don't be afraid of these things just because they're different. Some of these differences could change your life.

When you embrace diversity you'll even find

new ways to think, solve problems, and see the world around you.

LESSON N°. THIRTY:
Communicate, Communicate, and Communicate.

The quality of your communication is the quality of your life. —*Anthony Robbins*

In this world, conflict is everywhere. I do believe we need to approach conflict head-on, but my first choice would be to not have conflict in the first place. The number one source of conflict? Lack of communication.

In order to have successful relationships, you need to communicate.

Communication is a tool that must be used positively to do a lot of good for a business or relationship. Conversely, a lack of communication will create fear, uncertainty, and lack of trust.

Communication is essential to all relationships, in business and personally. In my relationship with my wife Robin, poor communication on my part has been the greatest source of conflict in our 30 years of marriage.

Forbes calls communication, "Today's Most Important Skill". In my experience I've seen this proven true over and over again.

In the dozens of businesses I've owned and operated, communication has always been the top request of employees. In company-wide surveys, employees always comment that they wish they were communicated with more. People want to know what is going on around them. It creates a sense of security.

A brand-new company took on their first project and hired an employee to help complete it. As she worked on the project, she began to wonder what would happen to her after it was finished. When she was hired, she did not receive clear communication about her future when the project was completed. She spent weeks wondering, doubting, thinking about other jobs, and worrying about the intentions of her boss.

One day, she simply asked her boss. Their conversation lasted no longer than an hour, but clarified her role in the business and helped her feel confident and secure. She left wondering why she hadn't asked for clarity earlier.

Communicating could have saved her weeks of worrying.

Don't think you need to know all the answers to communicate. Sometimes it's important to communicate that you don't know. Communication in these situations brings clarity and security.

The best communicator almost always has the greatest influence.

If you're confused, clarify. Always over-communicate rather than under-communicate. It will save you from unnecessary stress, worry and frustration.

LESSON Nº. THIRTY-ONE:
Tell the Truth.

Before us lies two paths—honesty and dishonesty.
The shortsighted embark on the dishonest path; the
wise on the honest. —Napoleon Hill

Honesty is the foundation of good character—yet it's a hard trait to maintain. Why? Because lying can be easy, and it's tempting to avoid telling the truth to make ourselves look better.

But lying destroys relationships.

When your lies are found out, it becomes hard for other people to trust you. I think we've all been here. And there's nothing you can do take it back, the only option you have is to slowly regain trust.

When you lie, you also lose the respect of those around you.

I've seen many relationships ruined this way. Trust and respect are easy to lose, but hard to rebuild. Lying isn't worth this sacrifice.

Lying will not only destroy your relationships with others, but will also hurt you personally. If you've ever lied, you know the feeling. As soon as the words escape your mouth, your heart drops. There's a brief moment of terror wondering if they can see straight through your words. In the aftermath, depending on the lie, the guilt and shame will consume you.

You should always tell the truth to avoid these awful, uncomfortable situations.

But I know you're not perfect, and sometimes, you might tell a lie. After telling a lie, the shame of admitting it can feel worse than riding out the consequences that follow. But I promise you, it's not. If you make a mistake and lie, please, be honest. Admit your fault. One lie will always take more lies to cover up, and once you start a pattern of dishonesty, you'll have a hard time recognizing the truth.

We lie because we think it will make us look better and potentially save us from the consequences of the truth. Your appearance is so much less important than the truth. At the end of your life, your character will mean everything; your appearance will mean nothing.

I'm telling you this because I've been there. There was a time in my life when my appearance was more important to me than the truth, and that's hard to admit. But I would rather admit it almost destroyed my life than have you fall into the same trap.

Although it is hard to admit when you're wrong, I have found people respect you and honor the truth, even in situations where you hurt them.

LESSON Nº. THIRTY-TWO:
Be Generous.

> *Happy is the person whose life is ordered around giving rather than receiving.* —Andy Stanley

When I was a college student, I wondered what on earth I had to give to others. I knew about generosity, but I thought the rules didn't apply when you were a poor college student. You may have seen this chapter title and wondered the same thing.

The thing is, being generous has very little to do with your financial standing.

Generosity is a mindset. You always have something to offer and the ability to be generous with something. God has entrusted us with resources and we have an obligation to be the best steward we can be.

No matter how much or how little money you have, you can generously share your time, your talent, and your treasures.

Recognize that your time is also a valuable

resource you can be generous with. You have the ability to mentor someone else with your time, or volunteer at a local homeless shelter. Use your time to be generous and bless others.

Your talent is another way you have been entrusted. If you're good at math, you have the ability to help or tutor someone else. Are you great at cooking? Teach someone else who wants to learn. Always be open to the possibility to help others with the things you know and are good at.

Then there's money. Being generous with what you have is important. We often let our fear of not having enough money keep us from being generous at all. Although that can be a healthy fear, don't let it stop you from helping others. The gesture of buying someone a cup of coffee can go a long way.

You have been entrusted with much, and therefore bear a great responsibility. The more generous you are, the more you will be entrusted with.

Being generous is one of the most rewarding lessons I have learned. The opportunity to change another person's life or to simply lend a helping hand generates a feeling of overwhelming gratitude. The joy that comes with being generous is priceless.

LESSON Nº. THIRTY-THREE:
Manage Time Wisely.

Don't waste your life, make it count. —*Jim Moye, Jr.*

If you're like me, you've spent most of your younger years waiting to be older. You want to be tall enough to ride the ride, old enough to drive, stable enough to live on your own. When you're young, time seems to drag by, going on forever.

Time is never something you can create more of, and when you waste it, it's gone. There are only 24 hours in every day and only seven days a week. So if you want to be successful and reach your goals, you'll need to manage your time wisely.

The things you spend the majority of your time on will reflect what you truly care about. Know what you value and make sure you manage your time accordingly.

Ask yourself: **Am I spending my time on the right things?**

As you evaluate how your values are reflected in the way you spend your time, take advantage of all the time management resources that exist. The internet is full of tips and tricks to help you manage your time.

What you do need to know about your time is you'll most likely take it for granted. You're not promised to live a long life, and although I hope you do, I need you to know you might not. It's a sobering idea that the time you have now is limited. But I hope by realizing this, you see how important it is to manage your time.

The more years that pass by, the faster they seem to go. Suddenly you'll find yourself wishing just maybe you could slow time back down. There are so many things you'll want to do and dreams you'll want to accomplish.

Make the most of it.

LESSON N°. THIRTY-FOUR:
Listen.

*Listen twice before you speak once. —Scottish
Proverb*

"Hey, what do you think of that email I sent you?" asks the boss.

"Oh, well actually I had some thoughts about what you said about…" the employee pauses as she notices her boss starting to look at his phone, "the…"

A few seconds later, noticing the pause, the boss perks back up, "Oh, what was that you said?"

"Nothing…" and the employee walks away.

You've probably experienced situations like this before.

When someone feels you aren't listening to them it hurts. They feel like either their thoughts aren't important or you don't care. Either way, this will really damage your relationships. Your friends will be less likely to speak up in the future;

your failure to listen has damaged their trust.

Listening is an important skill to help you develop deep relationships and gain people's trust. It shows you are interested in the people around you. Listening can be even more important than speaking. Conversely, failing to listen to others will hurt those around you and ultimately yourself.

Listening comes naturally to some. For most people, though, it's a learned skill. So don't feel bad if you're not good at listening, but don't feel stuck, either. You can develop the skill of being a good listener. So next time you're with someone, why not practice this skill and instead of talking, ask and listen.

You should be listening twice as much as you speak. It is a skill you need professionally and personally that will make or break your relationships with others. Remember, the most important person is the one in front of you.

LESSON Nº. THIRTY-FIVE:
Find a Mentor (or Several).

There is no lack of knowledge out there, just a shortage of people asking for help.

Imagine you're driving through an unfamiliar city. You have a meeting to get to and the traffic going that direction is crazy. You've also heard rumors this city is notorious for giving tickets and you wish you knew what part of town to avoid. Sound stressful?

What if in that moment you met someone who had lived in the city for years? Someone who knew how to get around the traffic, avoid the tickets, and even find a good place to park?

Which scenario would you rather face: struggling to get to your meeting alone or following the person who's been doing it for years? Obviously, the best option is to follow the person who knows what they're doing.

The answer seems so clear in driving directions. So why do we act like it is any different in life?

The pressure to figure out how to be successful and have good, strong relationships can be overwhelming, and often we feel like we need to do it all on our own. That's just not true. You will never know what you don't know, and the best way to figure it out is to have someone who has already been there help you. No amount of "how-to" books or "self-help" articles can ever fill in the gap a mentor can.

The fastest way to grow and get where you want to go in life is to surround yourself with people who have already gone the distance. Finding a mentor is vital to a successful life.

In my life I've been mentored by several people. Some people have given me valuable advice on starting and running a business, while others have focused on mentoring me in my relationships and spiritual life. Jim Moye mentored me in all of these areas. His insight and advice as someone who had already accomplished what I was trying to do has been irreplaceable.

Find someone you are willing to trust and who is willing to invest in your life.

LESSON Nº. THIRTY-SIX:
Write Thank You Notes.

Appreciation can make a day—even change a life. Your willingness to put it into words is all that is necessary. —Margaret Cousins

When I was young, my mom made me write thank you notes after every birthday party and Christmas. I'd sit at the kitchen table rapidly scribbling on a notepad the same few sentences over and over, changing just the names and the gifts I was thankful for. Your parents may have made you do the same—and if you're like me, you probably grumbled about it, wondering why in the world it was so important.

I never realized the value in what I was doing until I was older, but now I've seen these simple thank you notes make huge impressions on those around me.

It's one thing to be grateful, but it's completely

different to actually express gratitude. The act of expressing gratitude will change your life and the lives of others.

The art of writing thank you notes has largely been lost in our society. Because these notes are so rare, the effect they have on the recipient is actually much greater. Receiving a handwritten note can make someone feel affirmed and appreciated.

A thank you note might be the difference between getting a job or not. Often, surprised by the note, a potential employer will take a second look. It could even be the difference in creating meaningful relationships, making a difference in the life of a friend.

Writing thank you notes doesn't take long, but the effect they carry will take you a long way. Develop this habit and watch the impact it will have on your life, relationships, and those around you.

LESSON N°. THIRTY-SEVEN:
Be Present.

In everything you do, be fully present in the
moment. —*Unknown*

As a people, we are severely distracted. It's a rare thing for a person's thoughts to allow them to stay in the present moment.

One of the major things that keeps people distracted and distant is technology. In order to keep connected, the majority of the population is constantly texting, uploading pictures, and updating Facebook statuses. Despite good intentions, the methods of staying connected have begun to tear us apart.

You can't go anywhere without noticing most people glued to their phones. Around the dinner table, while walking outside, even some while driving, their minds constantly preoccupied with something else. Instead of focusing on family or friends, so many people are too busy scrolling and tapping the small devices in their hands.

When you live like this you start missing out on the life that's right in front of you. You continue going through the motions while forgetting or neglecting where you actually are. It's dangerous. The consequences of living a life like this are shallow relationships and missing out on the beauty of life around you.

In my more than forty years of life, the most impactful and meaningful things in my life have been relationships and experiences. The only way I've developed those relationships and had those experiences, though, has been through **being fully present**.

There's a difference between physically sitting somewhere and really being present in the moment. Sitting across from a friend and occasionally staring at the sky and checking your phone isn't being present. Being present looks like asking good questions and looking into their eyes. It's breathing deeply and taking in your surroundings.

The first step to becoming present in the moment is to become fully aware of where you are and who you're with. It's turning your phone off and making the most of where you are.

Regardless of where you are in a moment, life will keep moving on around you. It's a hard thing to sit in the moment you are in, while neglecting for just a moment the thoughts pulling you to any place but where you are.

The text or tweet you send won't last, but you

will value the connections you make with people for the rest of your life.

If you want to look back on a life well lived, learn to be present where you are.

LESSON Nº. THIRTY-EIGHT:
Master the Fundamentals.

Get the fundamentals down and the level of everything you do will rise. —*Michael Jordan*

One of my business partners played professional baseball for 11 years. Adam was small in comparison to a lot of the other players and therefore didn't have the speed, strength, or size most everyone else had in his profession. What he did to deal with this problem was to master the fundamentals.

He practiced tirelessly to master the basic skills of baseball, and he did. When the time came for him to make important plays he was prepared and performed well. As a result of his mastery of the fundamentals, he became the starting shortstop.

Most sports teams focus tirelessly on fundamentals and basics as well.

If athletes seek to master the basics before tackling the bigger plays, why don't we do the same in our lives?

To live a successful life, you have to master the fundamentals. The fundamentals are what make up who you are. Honestly, most of the lessons in this book are fundamentals. So before you start a huge business, or decide you're going to change the world, I urge you to make sure you know who you are.

Never believe if you are weak in one area you can't get better. Fundamentals are for building upon. Fundamentals are what is going to get you through hard situations that would otherwise break your foundation. Make sure your foundation is strong and that you are sure of who you are, what your values are, and where you want to be.

LESSON N°. THIRTY-NINE:
Live With Less.

Living on less creates the potential to do more.
—*Jeff Shinabarger*

It's easy to get sucked into the idea you need the newest and nicest things. And even if you don't buy into that, you will probably still find yourself living with a lot more than you necessarily need.

As I've traveled around the world and worked with people who had significantly less, I never noticed they were any less happy. In fact most of the time they were more joyful. So often you think the amount you possess directly correlates with how happy you will be, but it never does.

No amount of material possessions will satisfy you. In fact, living with less allows you to focus more on the people and experiences around you, and those are the things that will really impact your life.

I'm not saying material possessions are

necessarily bad. The bigger idea is that living in the constant pursuit of gaining more is going to destroy you. I've seen the long-term consequences of an insatiable hunger for more stuff. Too many of my friends' marriages have ended in divorce and family strife because of this "need" for more. I want stronger, deeper, more fulfilling things for you. The things people are chasing after are never worth the consequences they find themselves with.

Be grateful for what you have and don't feel compelled to keep up appearances with what the rest of the world and even your friends or family might have.

When possible, live with less and spend less. You might just find the less you actually have, the more space you have for the things that really matter.

LESSON N°. FORTY:
Admit Your Faults.

There is no better test of a man's integrity than his behavior when he is wrong —Marvin Williams

Honestly, this has been one of the hardest lessons for me to learn. I hate to admit it, but I had to learn this one the hard way before it really sunk in.

You have to realize your way might not always be the right way, regardless of what you think. You will be wrong, and you need to be okay with that.

I learned this lesson best through my marriage. Many times throughout the years I've thought I was right about something and fought over and over again to prove I was right. Not only was I often wrong, but as I tried desperately to prove I was right, my relationship with my wife suffered.

It is easy to get wrapped up in thinking you're right and lose sight of the people you might hurt in the process. Pride is always involved in this and you have to learn to put it aside.

The first step to mending relationships and getting over these prideful hurdles is to admit your faults.

Learning to admit your faults goes against all of our human instincts. It's something you have to consciously choose to do. It's a hard thing to do, and the growth process will take time. But the consequences of not learning it are severe. When you are wrong, always admit it—to yourself and others.

As you continually choose to admit when you're wrong, you'll develop a teachable, humble spirit.

Humility is amongst the top desired leadership traits. And as you learn to be humble, you will be trusted more by others. There is always something different about someone who openly admits when they were wrong. Their honesty is refreshing, and do you know the best part? When someone admits their faults, they will learn from their failures.

If we seek to learn instead of insisting on how "right" we are, we will find ourselves constantly improving our abilities, leadership skills, and developing deep relationships that come out of humble conversations.

We all have faults and shortcomings. If you admit those faults when you come across them, you'll be surprised by how your humility will impact others.

LESSON Nº. FORTY-ONE:
Small Problems, Big Picture.

Don't sweat the small stuff. —*Richard Carlson*

Flat tires, speeding tickets, broken computers, cancelled flights, lost paychecks. In the moment, a little problem can feel like the end of the world, ruining our days and derailing our plans.

But life is too short to lose sleep and relationships over small problems.

I was once involved in a huge business deal, a transaction totaling over 23-million-dollars. As we were getting ready to close the deal the seller presented two demands valued at a few thousands of dollars. In the midst of the 23-million-dollar deal, these seemed insignificant. But the seller became so fixated on these small points that the deal as a whole was put in jeopardy. Those small problems almost caused the entire deal to fall apart.

So many people get upset about the smallest

things, even I do sometimes. But compared to the big picture, these small problems really are insignificant.

What's the big picture? It's the long-range view—your life plans, goals, and dreams. You will always encounter problems, setbacks, and bumps in the road. The key is to asses if the problems you are facing are really going to impact the big picture.

More often than not, that flat tire isn't *really* going to ruin your life. Therefore, it's not worth the stress and upset that letting it consume you will cause.

Don't let these small details that you will come across ruin your days and take all your focus. Instead, remember what is important and what the big picture is and how you can work toward that.

In the moment, you'll be tempted to let these small problems consume you, but remember how much you have to be thankful for and don't let such small inconveniences steal your joy.

Don't sweat the small stuff. Remember the greater picture and focus your efforts accordingly.

LESSON Nº. FORTY-TWO:
Don't Complain.
Be the Change.

Be the change that you want to see in the world.
—Mahatma Gandhi

I was recently told a story by a friend who had been traveling the world on a year-long mission trip. He looked back to a time he was in a remote village in Thailand. It was the hot season and temperatures stayed in the 100s with high humidity. The electricity was sparse and therefore so was any use of fans. Most days he was served slimy lettuce with cold rice for breakfast, lunch, and dinner. His job? To go into huge fields of rice and spread manure on them—by hand.

From the start, he and his team found ample reason to complain.

A few days in, the whole team was miserable, exhausted, and growing resentful. Then my friend realized the real root of this problem: complaining had consumed their thoughts and changed their outlook on the situation.

Continuing to complain would not improve their situation—it was actually making it worse. So when their griping made life almost unbearable, they decided to make a change: to work harder and make the best of the situation.

As soon as they did this, their entire outlook changed.

You'll find yourself in a lot of difficult situations throughout your life. In those times, complaining looks like the easy way out, but in reality, it's the worst thing you can do. Complaining doesn't get you anywhere but working harder to solve the problem at hand will.

Working hard to solve problems in front of you will be the difference between enjoying life and moving forward or potentially staying stuck and bitter. To stop complaining is much more valuable to you and the others around you. Instead, try solving the problem and take action. Sometimes, the situation won't change, but the way you view and experience something can.

Despite your circumstance, you are in control of how you approach a problem. Take action. Create impact instead of complaining and the way you view and experience the problem will be transformed. **Be the change.**

Conclusion.

I want this book to be more than pages filled with stories and lessons telling you how to live your life. I want it to help guide you so you can live a life you want to live. The advice in this book circles around this central idea: your life really is what you make it. And your life is meaningless if you don't actually use it. A fulfilling life is all about intentionality.

The knowledge and intellect contained in this book are actually of little value without action. Anyone can listen or read a book but taking action is far more valuable. Applied learning is a much better teacher, even if you end up failing. The people who take action and risks in applying the different lessons in this book are the leaders who will rise up and change your generation and the ones to come. They are the leaders in a family, job, church and community.

My hope is instead of listing all these pieces of advice in expectancy that you will change how you live, you will instead just begin to see your life and potential impact differently. You really do have the ability to assess all aspects of your life and begin to make changes that can help you achieve your dreams. Know yourself to lead yourself. Live your life with intention and you will be pleasantly surprised by the results.

Don't just sit back and let life come to you by accident. This is your life, live it well.

I will leave you with a poem I wrote to Barrett, my son, when he was 10 years old, and more importantly, the poem he wrote in response 8 years later when he was first heading to college:

Live your life always giving your best,
Let your effort be the test.
It is not always the results that matter in the end,
But the path you take that reflects within.
If you keep your cool in good times and bad
And press onward, you will usually be glad.
To live with integrity you must learn to trust
You will be betrayed, but keep faith in others you must.
Reach for the stars and imagine big dreams,
And keep your faith with all crumbles it seems.
You must take risks to reap big gains,
Remember this always as you experience life's pains.
Seek the advice of trusted advisors and friends,

They can help you determine what's around life's next
bend.
Sometimes it is not easy ignoring what people say,
But run from foolish people, let wisdom guide your
way.
Let your heart be guided by our God from above,
And leave in your tracks faith, hope, and love.
Our world needs leaders and I know God has a plan,
For you to grow from a boy and be a successful man.

In August 2012, he wrote this response.

Dad, you have always taught me to give my all,
And my prayer today is that it will reflect this Fall.
I have learned that the scoreboard holds no true value,
But it is in a good attitude that others will see virtue.
Perseverance has led me to 'fight the good fight',
And oh the joys of victory when defeating the night!
Many times it has been difficult to trust and not judge,
But from now on I hope to never again hold a grudge.
Going from dreams, to goals, to finally decisions of
faith,
You have laid my foundation, now it's time to
accelerate.
We've tried a lot of new things together, even wild-
hearted at times,
Especially para-gliders, gunshots, and rocky mountain
climbs.

You have always been my mentor and coach, my father
and friend;

Your love and your guidance I will always cherish
within.

Society and culture are only here trying to capture the
mind,

But know that the rock of Christ's wisdom is to which
I will bind.

My soul is convicted to live completely for God's love,

And I refuse to ever settle for anything less than His
path above.

As this poem comes to a close, please receive the
thankfulness of my heart,

For no longer am I a boy, but because of you, living as
a successful man I will start.

Bonus Content.

I want this book to be more than paper and ink. In order to do that, I've compiled some of my best articles, life lessons, and resources online! The information on the site will help you apply everything you've read about. Find more here: www.decideyourdestination.com.

Sign up online to receive more information and free updates. Online you will also find a free, short quiz that will help you determine what your values are and how they can change your life (www.decideyourdestination.com/quiz)."

A Note from the Author

If you have been encouraged by the life lessons in this book and would like to share it with others, here are some ideas and easy ways to help:

Leave a review and your thoughts on Amazon.com.

I know many of you have blogs, Facebook pages & Twitter accounts. I'd love to have you post a review of the book along with a link to www.decideyourdestination.com. Your recommendation is all that many will need to pick up the book. All proceeds from the book will go to the Impact 2:52 Foundation which focuses on youth education & organizations which provide a positive Impact on the lives of others.

Check out the blog.

I will be blogging on www.decideyourdestination.com & www.impact252.com on a regular basis. Come by and check it out. I hope to have plenty of stories to tell. Please leave me a comment with your story or any life lessons.

Connect on Social Media.

Be my friend on Facebook, my personal page or Impact 2:52. I would love to connect and stay in touch. I am a little less active, but have accounts on LinkedIn, Twitter & Instagram as well.

Buy a few copies to give away.

Remember all proceeds go to charity. I have a friend who gave a copy to all her employees and another to all the seniors in her son's class. If you have a school, ministry or other organization who would like to order in bulk, please contact me.

Book me for speaking.

If you have an opportunity to speak at your organization, conference, church or school, send me an email at chad@impact252.com and I will see what I can arrange. I love to talk about being intentional, leadership, entrepreneurship and sharing lessons from my journey.

My hope and prayer is that I can help others live with intentionality, purpose & authenticity. Thank you for reading this book, I hope it helped in some small way. And, thanks for your part in passing along the opportunity to others. Discover your values, define your mission and Be Intentional!

Contact Me

Send me a note:

Chad Merrill

P.O. Box 49212

Atlanta, GA 30359

Email me:

chad@impact252.com

Call me:

404-245-3959

Made in the USA
Columbia, SC
07 September 2017